Copyright © 2021 Andrew Listvinsky

All rights reserved.

ISBN: 9798543176801

Acknowledgements

To David Moss, LCSW, for sharing your feedback and wisdom with me. For helping me to learn my value and gain confidence in my abilities. For being as mentor I am proud to look up to.

To Dr. Michael Majeski, for giving me the confidence to share my writing. For being a guide and teacher who inspires me to grow both in skill and in kindness.

To Dr. Matthew Herbert, for sharing his passion and experience with a young college student who had more curiousity than sense of direction.

To my parents and my friends, for your encouragement, feedback, and love.

"If you've seen one therapist, you've seen one therapist." -Dr. Matthew Herbert

Key Points

- <u>Your therapist should</u>: Be licensed. Inform you of the limits of confidentiality. Help you express yourself. Help you look at things in new ways. Encourage change. Collaborate with you. Show you that they care. More information on page 9.

- <u>Your therapist should NOT</u>: Behave in a sexual manner towards you. Have any other role in your life. Accept expensive gifts. More information on page 20.

- <u>All therapists are different</u>: Some tend to be leaders who provide more direct feedback. Some tend to be followers who encourage you to develop your independence. Individual personality makes a big difference. No two therapists are exactly alike. More information on page 24.

- <u>Progress in therapy</u>: Looks different for each person. Has many forms. Can take longer depending on the problems you face and how engaged you are. More information on page 26.

Introduction

Finding the right therapist is not always a simple task. It's tempting to say that any therapist that has the right license, training, and experience will be able to help you with your particular mental health, relationship, or life issues. Those are all important things to look for in a therapist. However, it is essential that you as the client have a good relationship with your therapist. Therapy often involves diving into intimate thoughts and feelings in order to make progress. It is much more difficult to make headway when for whatever reason you feel unable to discuss these heavy topics with your therapist. Since your relationship with the therapist influences treatment so much, the therapy experience will be very different depending on who your therapist is.

Therapy has historically been made out to be a mysterious process, which is both untrue and unhelpful. Fortunately, therapists of the last few decades have come to realize that transparency is far more beneficial than asking clients to put their faith in a process they don't understand. In keeping with that spirit, it is my hope that this booklet helps pull back the curtains and can assist those in therapy or considering therapy to make informed decisions. This booklet will lay out some important ways of determining whether a therapist is right for you.

Lastly, I wish to preface that the contents of this

booklet primarily apply to "outpatient psychotherapy."

Outpatient therapy means that you attend your

therapy session either virtually or in person at a

designated time, and then depart until your next

scheduled appointment. If you are in an intensive

outpatient program or receiving therapy in a

residential treatment setting, please take that into

account. If you are part of a structured mental health or

recovery program, your various therapy providers may

have different roles in your treatment.

Identifying Good Therapy

Here are some questions that may have crossed your mind as you engage in therapy or as you consider starting therapy.

Who is a qualified therapist?

There are people in the U.S who advertise themselves as therapists, counselors, etc., but who have no formal training or qualifications. Aside from the lack of education and knowledge of how to provide mental health services, the bigger danger that working with such an individual creates is that there is no accountability. Qualified therapists are either licensed by a professional licensing board, or are directly overseen by a licensed therapist if they are in training.

Not only does the license indicate a certain level of competency, it also means that the therapist is held to a certain standard by the organization from which they got their license. If they don't meet those standards by acting inappropriately, you have the option of reporting them to their licensing board. Unethical behavior from a therapist means they could lose their license, their job, and their employability moving forward.

The names of licenses to practice therapy differ state-by-state, but generally include some variation of the following:

- Licensed Clinical Social Worker

- Licensed Clinical Counselor

- Licensed Clinical Psychologist

- Licensed Marriage and Family Therapist

In addition to the title, a licensed therapist will have a license number. Feel free to request your therapist's license number before you start treatment. You can look up this number in an online registry to determine whether their license is in good standing. For example, if your therapist is licensed in California, you can verify whether their license is valid through the Board of Behavioral Sciences or California Board of Psychology.

What should therapy look like?

What any given therapy session consists of will, of course, depend on you, your therapist, and the issues you wish to address. At the core of therapy is conversation. We tend to understand ourselves and our situations better when we are asked to express them to other people. But therapy is not just the process of you telling your life story, though that can certainly be part of it. There are many schools of thought when it comes to therapy, and many approaches borne out of those schools. However, even within all this variety there are certain qualities of good therapy that are universal.

Professionalism: Therapy is a professional service. As

such, therapists need to interact with their clients in a

professional manner. This means your relationship

with the therapist is clear and your contact with them

is generally limited to the therapy itself and logistics

such as scheduling. Unless there is an emergency,

therapy should not begin until you have been provided

with an informed consent document detailing the cost

of therapy, the therapist's policies for missed

appointments, and other important details. Either your

therapist or the agency they work for should answer

any questions you have about the informed consent

document.

Confidentiality: Arguably, the most valuable thing about

therapy is that what's discussed in therapy is largely confidential. With a few exceptions, your therapist must keep everything you say private. Records your therapist keeps must be kept in a secure place. Therapy relies on people feeling that they can discuss anything with little or no filtering. Your therapist should discuss the limits of confidentiality with you before starting treatment. Generally, therapists are obligated to break confidentiality if you pose an immediate risk of harm to yourself or someone else, if a child is abused, if an adult who depends on others to meet their needs is abused, or if a judge orders the therapist to release records to the court.

New ideas: There are many ways to accomplish this, but therapy should result in new views or approaches to tackling your problems. Sometimes this comes from the therapist teaching you new strategies, sometimes from you realizing something during a conversation with your therapist, and sometimes this comes unexpectedly while going about your day. People generally come to therapy having tried to solve their problems on their own. The perspective a therapist offers may result in solutions you hadn't considered.

Expression of emotion: Your therapy session should be a place where you can be honest about your emotions. Whether this means simply stating how you feel or crying, therapy should let you have a place to express yourself without fear of judgement. One of the oldest and best known truths of therapy is that a lot of healing can be done just from people being able to be honest about how they feel. The opportunity to break what may have been years of silence is often a great source of relief.

Action: Therapy is ultimately about changing something in your life. Since we can only control our own actions, this means finding new ways for you to interact with people and the world that can help make those changes reality. In other words, it's about changing your behavior. A good therapist will generally encourage you to do things differently and to deviate from your usual patterns. This could mean going out to meet new people to help with feelings of loneliness. It could mean splashing water on your face when you get angry to help you calm down. It could mean meditating to help you focus and identify your emotions. Most of the time, the goals you have in therapy are more likely to be reached if you practice the skills you learn in your life outside of the therapy session.

Collaboration: Treatment decisions and goals should be discussed between your therapist and yourself. This is not to say that you and your therapist need to be in agreement on everything. However, at the very least a general sense of your purpose in therapy should be clear for both of you since therapy involves work from both the therapist and yourself.

Client feedback is welcome: No therapist is perfect because no person is perfect. A good therapist knows that it's important to ask for feedback from their clients, and take what they say to heart. If you have concerns or questions about the therapy, your therapist should at least honor that feedback with a discussion, and by potentially making changes to the therapy. A good therapist will know that no matter how brilliant a treatment technique or strategy is, it will not necessarily work for every client.

Caring: Part of a therapist's job is to care about their clients. A good therapist will be able to find a way to care about most of their clients no matter what the client's history or life contains. This doesn't mean your therapist will be overjoyed by all of your decisions and qualities, but you should absolutely have the sense that they want you to get better. Naturally, therapists are human and there may be topics that are outside their skill set or comfort zone. A good therapist will be honest with you if they feel unable to provide you the assistance you're looking for.

What SHOULDN'T therapy look like?

These are red flags. If your therapy involves these things, leave and look for a new therapist. I would also encourage you to consider filing a report with your state's licensing board. To do this, you will want to have the therapist's license number. Every licensed therapist is aware that these behaviors are unacceptable and can cost them their license and career.

Sex and sexual advances: Therapy never involves sex between yourself and the therapist. Period. If your therapist behaves in a sexual way towards you, they are violating your rights and their code of ethics.

Unwanted physical touch: It's not uncommon for therapists to provide a hug or to hold the hand of a client to help them through a difficult time. Many people find a touch on the arm or other simple forms of physical contact to be helpful in bringing a sense of safety. However, some people find physical contact to be stressful. A good therapist may not immediately know your preference, but they will respect you if you say that you do not wish to be touched. If a therapist uses touch as a bigger part of their treatment style, it should be mentioned in their informed consent document and discussed with you during your first meeting.

Multiple relationships: Your therapist shouldn't have any other role in your life. In smaller towns or cities this may be more difficult, but it should always be the goal. Your therapist shouldn't also be your teacher, mechanic, employee, friend, etc. This is to avoid situations where something that happened during therapy influences how you or your therapist act towards each other outside of therapy (or vice versa). Your therapist may know things about you that no one else does, and this may cause you to fear how they might influence other parts of your life.

Accepting expensive gifts or tips: Though it is generally frowned upon by the therapy community, therapists accepting gifts from their clients is not always a bad

thing. Depending on your cultural background, it may

be important to you to offer people who help you a

gift. However, therapists should not encourage their

clients to give them gifts. Most importantly, gifts of

large monetary value should never be accepted by

your therapist. If it's important for you to give your

therapist a gift for the holidays or any other occasion, I

strongly encourage providing them something you

made yourself. Whether it's a small handmade blanket,

cookies, or some vegetables from your own garden,

something that holds more emotional value than

monetary value will be much more readily accepted.

Why do I feel like my therapist says too much/little?

One of the most common complaints I hear from people about their therapist is "they just sit there!" or "they never tell me what I should do." From time to time, I also hear "they talk to me like they know my life better than I do!" or "I wish they'd ask me what I thought about their instructions."

Therapists vary in how much they direct the course of the therapy session. Therapists who tend to be leaders are more likely to propose solutions or teach skills. Therapists who are followers tend to let the client decide the topic of any given therapy session, and encourage their client to find their own solutions through discussing the problem. Most therapists switch between leading and following depending on the situation. Even so, therapists will tend to lean one way or the other. Ideally their style matches what you're looking for. A therapist who sees their primary role as encouraging you to grow and become more independent may provide therapy that looks different from a therapist who sees their primary role as teaching you strategies for understanding and changing your thoughts and feelings.

It's important to consider whether you are looking for your therapist to be more of a leader or a follower. It can be helpful to ask your therapist what they consider their primary role in therapy to be.

Is therapy working?

A surprising number of people are hesitant to ask this question. But it's important to remember that at the end of the day, therapy is a professional service into which you are investing an incredible amount of of time and effort.

Whether therapy will work and how quickly depends on many things, not the least of which is how good a match a therapist is for you in terms of both personality and treatment style. Their experience in helping people with similar problems and their training will also play a role.

Another big factor that will determine the success of therapy is you, the client. Therapy is a team effort that requires work from both the therapist and

the client. Therapy is much more likely to be beneficial

if the client arrives to sessions on time, tries to apply

what they gain from therapy to their life, and shows up

to sessions ready to work on their challenges.

It's important to recognize that the kind of

problems you're tackling in therapy and how intensely

they affect you individually will also play a role in the

speed of progress. One person may attend therapy to

address their anxiety and learn how to manage it far

better in just a few sessions. For another it may take the

better part of a year. Another person may seek support

for the death of a loved one and continue to benefit

from seeing their therapist eight years later. If you've

come to therapy to take on problems that have been present for decades or that came from severe or repeat traumatic events, progress may only begin after a long period of learning to trust and open up to your therapist. It's difficult to heal a lifetime of injury in a manner of hours.

Therapy is not a linear process. Setbacks as well as bursts of progress are expected. There is no hard and fast rule for how long therapy should take or how soon into therapy you should start to see improvement. No two people's therapy process looks identical. However, you should not be afraid to talk to your therapist if you think that something about therapy isn't working. Regardless of whether you're uncertain about one detail of therapy or have concerns about about the entire process, I encourage you to share your thoughts with your therapist.

Improvement can take a lot of forms, and progress will look different depending on the issues that brought you into therapy. Areas of improvement can be broadly broken down into three categories: Feeling better, living the life you want, and having a better support system.

1) *Feeling better*: You're going to therapy because you're hoping to feel better. This can include wanting to feel less hopeless, anxious, paranoid,

angry, alone, etc. There are a few points I want to make about "feeling better." First, therapy often entails feeling worse before feeling better. You're coming face to face with difficult topics, mistakes you've made, or injustices done to you by others. In order to address a problem, you initially have to learn more about it, and this typically brings sadness as you come to recognize the task ahead of you. Second, people sometimes don't realize how much better they are doing. This is because the improvement is gradual, and is easier for an outsider (such as a friend or your therapist) to recognize than yourself. But what may be the biggest pitfall is that many people go into therapy with the

expectation that someday they will never have

to experience any of those bad feelings ever

again. Some believe things are only "better" if

all the bad feelings are gone for good. If you find

yourself with this mindset going into therapy, I

encourage you to discuss it with your therapist.

Whether you're going to therapy with serious

mental health issues/trauma or seeking support

to help you navigate a rough patch in your life,

we all experience the full range of human

emotions (including the ones we don't enjoy).

2) *Living the life you want:* Therapists (including

myself) will sometimes ask their clients to describe how their life would be different if the problem just magically disappeared. Often this is used as a way to help our clients identify their motivation for coming to therapy and tackling their problems. However, even more important than that, it helps answer the question of "what's next?" If someone with depression stops feeling incredible sadness, lack of self-worth, exhaustion, or whatever combination of symptoms they're struggling with, they can still just as easily spend all day in bed and isolate themselves from the world until they are miserable again. Feeling better gives you an opportunity to create a domino effect that will

make sure the improvements don't end when

therapy does.

3) *A better support system:* As I've mentioned,

therapy is not always an enjoyable process. I

encourage my clients to take some time after the

session (if possible) to themselves or with a

trusted friend to help them get back into a head

space where they can take on whatever tasks

come next that day. However, if you don't have

people you can lean on for support when you're

going through emotional turmoil, that's often

the best place for your therapy to start. The

more difficult the topic of therapy or the more

painful it is for you to experience unpleasant

emotions, the more important it will be to start

by making sure you have at least a few people

you can rely on to help you bounce back from

tough days. We also know that healing works

best when paired with connection. Your

connection with your therapist can help you

learn to form healthy relationships with others.

Conclusion

For those of you who are considering therapy or have just started therapy, remember that all therapists are different because all people are different. Somebody who is considered an amazing friend by one person may be considered incredibly annoying to another. Therapy will be very different depending on who you're working with. I've heard too many people say "I guess therapy isn't for me" after one bad experience. It can certainly be disheartening to seek help for the first time and not find what you're looking for. I urge you to keep looking.

This booklet opens with a quote from one of my first mentors, "If you've seen one therapist, you've seen one therapist." As someone who has been through the journey of finding the right therapist for myself, I firmly believe that not only is this true, but that taking the time to find a therapist who understands you and your goals makes a world of difference. You will find the right therapist for you. When you do, I hope you stop and recognize that you've already made a huge step in your healing journey.

<u>**Helpful Resources**</u>

-211: Dial 211 anywhere in the U.S. (including all 50

states, Puerto Rico, and the Distric of Columbia) to be

connected to your local social services. They can

provide referrals and information regarding many

community services including therapy for those with

lower incomes.

-Psychology Today: The website

www.psychologytoday.com is one of the largest

listings of therapists in the U.S. It allows you to sort by

categories such as insurance and specialities.

-National Crisis Line: Dial 800-273-8255 anywhere in the

U.S to be connected to a crisis counselor 24/7 who can

help you through thoughts of suicide, and other crises.

They also provide referrals and information to help you find mental health services in your area.

-*Crisis Text Line*: Text "Home" to 741-741 or go to www.crisistextline.org to speak with a crisis counselor via text or messenger. This option is especially useful for those who can't find the privacy to call a crisis phone line.

www.ingramcontent.com/pod-product-compliance
Lightning Source LLC
Chambersburg PA
CBHW061545250726

48657CB00006B/2297